OUTRAGEOUS QUESTIONS

LEGACY OF BRONSON ALCOTT AND AMERICA'S ONE-ROOM SCHOOLS

BY

LAURIE JAMES

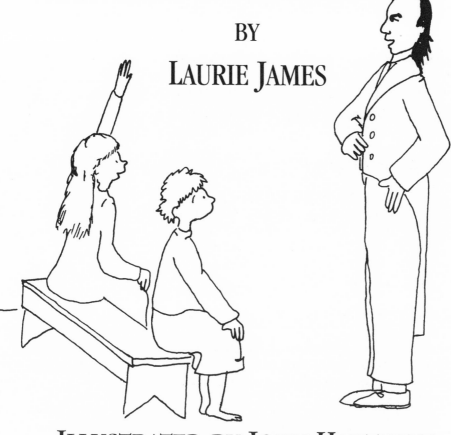

ILLUSTRATED BY JOHN HARTNETT

GOLDEN HERITAGE PRESS, INC.
NEW YORK

Golden Heritage Press, Inc., Suite 25D, 500 West 43rd Street, New York, NY 10036

Designer and Compositor: Richard Scillia, Creative Abilities, Wantagh, New York.

Publisher's Cataloging in Publication
James, Laurie.
     Outrageous questions : legacy of Bronson Alcott and America's one-room schools / by Laurie James ; illustrated by John Hartnett.
     p. cm.
     SUMMARY: Discusses the legacy of American one-room school education and Bronson Alcott's innovations to that legacy.
     Preassigned LCCN: 93-077360.
     ISBN 0-944382-05-3 paperback
     ISBN 0-944382-06-1 hardcover

     1. Alcott, Amos Bronson, 1799-1888–Juvenile literature. 2. Education–United States–History–Juvenile literature. 3. Education, Rural–United States–History–Juvenile literature.
     I. Hartnett, John, ill. II. Title.

LB695.A32J36 1993   370.92
                                     QBI93-687

Printed in the United States of America.
First Edition.

This book is dedicated
to those boys and girls
who never heard of
one-room schoolhouses.

ACKNOWLEDGEMENTS

THANKS TO...

Gwen Harper, Mary James, Erica Rosenast, Laurie Perkin, Cicely Sullivan,
Clifton James, Constance Fuller Threinen, Hardy James,
Lynn James-Gross, Waldron and Robert Schultz, Cynthia Weber, and
Ramona Barth, all of whom read the manuscript and offered
valuable advice and encouragement.

Maime Harper Rounds of Milwaukie, Oregon, for her oral history of her
experiences in attending and teaching in one-room schools in Oregon.

The Marysville, Kansas Chamber of Commerce for supplying
information and pictures of the one-room Bommer school.

Wayne E. Groner, Vice President for Development at Wayne State College,
and Sue Buryanek, Information Specialist at U. S. Conn Library for providing
information and pictures of the one-room country school in Wayne, Nebraska.

Jim Bergman, teacher and historian, for his knowledge of
The Center School in Alna, Maine.

Barbara Steele of Aberdeen, South Dakota, for sharing materials
she collected on one and two teacher schools in rural South Dakota.

TABLE OF CONTENTS

FOREWORD

Why do I believe this book should exist?

The first time I conducted Bronson Alcott's Conversation in a library workshop in Altus, Oklahoma, I was stunned. One after another, the questions were answered by twentieth century children exactly as had been answered by those living in 1836! I quivered with the impact of the realization that across a hundred and fifty years humanity remained the same.

Adults have been astounded with the results of this workshop. Since my first experience, groups of children have shown various responses and have displayed what I originally expected— keen wit, active imaginations, and energy.

I developed the workshop as part of my experience portraying the character of Margaret Fuller in the 1991-3[1] "American Renaissance" tour with The Great Plains Chautauqua Society, Inc., hosted and funded in part by thirty communities and made possible with major awards from The National Endowment on the Humanities Public and State Divisions and by NEH affiliates in Oklahoma, Kansas, Nebraska, South Dakota, and North Dakota.

Dressed as Margaret Fuller might have been when she taught in Bronson Alcott's Temple School in Boston in 1836, I described one-room schools and how children were educationally tracked in the early part of the nineteenth century. I compared this with Alcott's methods and ended with one of his Conversations. Since these were recorded by his assistants, Margaret Fuller and Elizabeth Peabody[2], and published, they are available to us today (*see Bibliography*). Therefore, at the end of the sessions I distributed his Conversation in pamphlet form, and let the youngsters compare our Conversation with what had taken place in that 1836 classroom.

Leading these sessions, I have observed that many contemporary children are not used to thinking inwardly or to reasoning because they do not hear these kinds of questions, nor do they think to ask them to themselves. Though most had difficulty articulating, I decided it was worthwhile to allow questions to sink in— in time the conversation might vex and bring about deeper perceptions.

It is extraordinary to watch give-and-take growing in a group. As both Socrates and Bronson Alcott understood, people of all ages can teach themselves through the art of a skilled questioner. In Huron, South Dakota when I asked an involved group at the end of the session what they had learned, one girl said— and she meant what she said — "A lot."

Two adults came up afterwards and commented on how interesting Alcott's method was. One said, "What a pity the children don't get more of this kind of teaching in school today. You see, they can learn like this – they can think on their own."

Many youngsters today have no conception of one-room country schoolhouses. They are charmed to hear about them and to visualize what it was like to go to school "in the old days." Most people I met in America's heartland are fully familiar with the structures – one woman listed the generations of her family, all of whom had attended the same little building over the course of a hundred years. I talked to some who had graduated from them, and quite a few who had taught in them. Everyone praised one-room schoolhouses, and there were those who wished they still operated. They still do operate in remote sections of our country, such as in eight rugged islands offshore Maine. On Matinicus Island, a fishing community, for instance, a one-room school generally enrolls from six to eleven students in all grade levels.

Numerous educators today advocate the return to the smaller, more personalized approach to learning. The inestimable advantages which seem to lose out in larger complexes are individualized attention, wholehearted friendliness, community spirit, informal atmosphere, stimulation and cooperation between age levels.

The generation that remembers those past, good days, along with their rich oral histories, is quickly vanishing. Our hats are tipped to schoolmasters and mistresses who, with limited facilities and training, used their intelligence and ingenuity to educate over a century of students. An innovative few, like Bronson Alcott, were strong enough to defy current practice and help to forge a path for new thinking.

Our red or white country schoolhouses are being trucked to restoration areas, repaired and repainted, turned into museums. It is important that we preserve them, visit them, experience their uniqueness. While we hail the benefits that modern educational methods and technology bring to the masses today, we need not forget to wax nostaglic about and to continue to emulate our meaningful values and roots of yesteryear.

Laurie James

AN OUTRAGEOUS MAN, HIS IDEAS, HIS SCHOOL.

AN OUTRAGEOUS SCHOOL was opened in Boston in the fall of 1834 by a gentle man whose name was Amos Bronson Alcott. He loved children, believed in their goodness, and felt that children should be put in touch with genius.

The Temple School was opened in one room in The Masonic Temple Hall in a city where new ideas were fermenting, and where writers and thinkers gravitated– the intellectual capital of the United States of America, Boston.

A Gothic window dominated. Over the door Alcott hung a sign that read "Universal Unity." He and his assistant, Elizabeth Peabody, placed pretty chairs around the room, and installed a long curved teacher's desk.

Courtesy of Concord Free Public Library
Source: After a sketch by Francis Graeter, Alcott's drawing master.

They hung pictures, maps, globes, and set up high pedestals with plaster casts of Jesus, Shakespeare, Plato, Milton, Scott. There was a statue of Atlas bearing the weight of the world on his shoulders, figurines of a child aspiring, a child reading, a child drawing, and a model of Silence, whose finger was raised as though saying, "Beware!"– which symbolized spiritual reality. They arranged geraniums and flowers on a shelf and put a green sofa near the stove. Thus, they were bringing the exterior or outward environment into harmony with the interior or outward spirit. They were cultivating the imagination and the heart.

To Alcott,

GENIUS WAS THE FREE-PLAY OF ALL THE FACULTIES OF A HUMAN BEING.

Genius was human nature rising superior to things and events.

It was the loftiest vision of truth and beauty.

Genius was only obscured by ignorance or evil.

The soul's growth would come through breathing the wisdom of the great.

Every person had the gems of perfection within, had self-initiating drives to find the divinity within.

Children, whose minds and energies were fresh to ideas, were closest to God, and could readily be awakened.

Needed was careful training to lead them to original thought.

Many people were outraged at Bronson Alcott's ideas because the prevailing thought was in concurrence that all human beings, including children, were sinful.

Finally Alcott was attacked by most parents as dangerous and heretical.

IT WAS THE NINETEENTH CENTURY…
YOU DID NOT HAVE TO GO TO SCHOOL…

even though some states in the U.S.A. had laws concerning education.[3] These laws were not enforced. If children were unhappy at school, they could leave and not return. The law stated that if children did not attend school, their parents were obliged to teach them to read.

Throughout America, there were public grammar schools – schools that taught both Latin and English grammar – and private academies in many cities.

You Were Lucky if You Went to School.

Most families lived in small villages or on farms. People used candles instead of electricity, woodstoves instead of central heating, horses instead of cars, and children could not always go to school because they were needed to help out on the farm or at home.

For instance, Abraham Lincoln totalled less than a year's schooling in his growing years. He lived on the frontier in Kentucky and Indiana, and school was four or five miles away. The nearby woods were full of wild animals, so he seldom made the daily walk. At night he read by the firelight and wrote his sums with a piece of charcoal on the back of a large wooden shovel or on the walls of his log cabin.

You Attended School Every Day
You Could Get There...

and probably you got there about two days out of every three.

Often extreme weather conditions, such as heavy snows, prevented you from hiking or riding your horse on dirt roads, or there weren't any roads. You made your way through fields and woods. Maybe there wasn't any school within walking distance.

Maime Harper, who lived in Corvallis, Oregon, remembers picking wildflowers on her way to school. If she got hungry, she stopped at a strawberry patch. "We had to pass one mean bull," she recalls. "You had to watch out for him. The man who owned him watched out for him too. My grandmother got attacked by him. As a matter of fact, if it hadn't been for a dog who chased that bull, the man who became my brother-in-law would have been dead today."

YOU WERE PRIVILEGED IF YOU ATTENDED SCHOOL, EVEN FOR A SHORT TIME.

Children born into poor families generally did not have the opportunity to go to school because they went to work with their parents in coal mines or factories where they labored up to sixteen hours per day, in order to bring in a few pennies for family support.[4]

If you were a negro,* you were forbidden schooling because you were to grow up to be a slave.[5] The law stated that teaching a slave to read and write was a crime punishable by death. One bright slave youngster, Frederick Douglass, learned to read when he met white children on the errands he ran for his master. He made friends with these boys and gave them bread (which he'd taken from his master's kitchen) if they'd explain and answer his questions. Frederick Douglass grew up to be a great leader, a writer, a newspaper editor, and an advocate for freedom of the slaves.

If you were born into a wealthy family, you would be taught by private tutors, as was George Washington, or if you lived on a plantation in the South you might very well be sent to England to be educated.

In many towns, parents pooled their moneys and rented a room in some building and furnished it with desks and benches. Or they built a wooden, one-room schoolhouse.

*In the nineteenth century, the accepted term for African-American was "negro" and therefore is used throughout this book when reference is within the context of this period of history.

In Colonial Days,
Schoolhouses Were Built of Logs...

cut from the nearby forest and windows were of paper greased with lard as a protection against rain. Roofs were of bark.

Inside, the floor was the bare earth which irritated your nose, eyes or legs when dusty, or sometimes the floor was made of puncheon, that is, rough timbers.

At one end of the room there would be a chimney of short logs daubed with clay.

Around the walls of the room sticks would be inserted between the logs and these sticks would hold up boards which served as desks.

Benches were backless, made of ax-hewn slabs which rested on wooden posts.

The master would have a chair and desk on which he kept a bunch of goose quills for the making of pens. Slates did not come into use until the 1820's and lead pencils were not available until some years later.

Not infrequently students heard the howls of wolves as they recited lessons, and sensed roving bands of Indians that roamed the edge of the woods.

As towns became more populated, the community elected a committee of selectmen who divided the area into districts and voted on where the schoolhouses should be built– always on land that could not be used for any other purpose. These selectmen determimed the money needed, assessed and apportioned taxes, chose masters, fixed salaries, and saw that the schools were inspected.[6]

These later schoolhouses, made of rough clapboard, were painted red, white, yellow, or grey. They had up to five or six small windows, plank floors, a shingled roof, a bell tower, and the walls were lathed and plastered.

Inside was the cast iron wood-burning stove, a hanging oil lamp, a pail with water and dipper, a blackboard (after 1820), a dictionary, a world globe, a map of the United States. There was a pine or oak table or desk for the teacher, sometimes on a platform. There were wooden benches of two different heights– one for older children and one for smaller children.

In the back of the school down a well worn path, there were two outhouses, one for boys, one for girls. Outhouses were small shed-like buildings some distance away from the school yard for the purpose of going to the toilet. There were no flush toilets. A hole was dug deep in the ground and a wooden seat or bench was constructed to fit over it.

There Were No Better Schools...
If You Had a Good Teacher.

Unfortunately, not many schools had good teachers.

Parents hired a teacher who would board with one of the neighboring families. This was a man or woman. He might be a graduate of Harvard, the leading college in America.

More often than not, the teacher was as young as sixteen, a person good at figures, who could read the Bible without stumbling over long words, who could write, mend a pen, assert authority and severity, for student obedience was considered a priority. But whoever this person was, he or she would have had no teacher training for there were no schools that trained teachers.

Generally, men teachers were paid more than women teachers.

When the teacher called on you, you had to stand and "toe the crack"– that is, line your toes up with a tiny opening between the floor boards.

SCHOOL WAS LIKE A BIG FAMILY.

The teacher made the fire, swept the floor, carried in the water – and might assign some chores to the older children.

Girls helped to open the school by cleaning and sweeping while boys chopped wood and made small repairs. The winter term often began the Monday after Thanksgiving.

You brought your lunch to school. In the cold winter you had to eat a cold lunch. One teacher, Maime Harper, had the idea to make hot soup every day. She brought in a big round pot and set up a rotating schedule so that students brought the ingredients from home every week.

ALL GRADE LEVELS
WERE TAUGHT IN THE SAME ROOM.

Your teacher promoted you to the next highest grade whenever you were considered ready. If you attended eight years, you would graduate.

The older children helped and stimulated the younger ones and vice versa. Smart lower grade youngsters listened to the lessons of the upper grade level and learned them. If you misbehaved, it was likely your own brother or sister who told your parents on you.

The school was the meeting place and social center of the community. Here everyone assembled for a political debate, an art exhibition, a song concert, or other activity. One big gala was the school Christmas program in which every student played a part.

In large towns the school ran almost continuously, but in small towns the winter term ran about ten or twelve weeks for older children, with a summer term of equal length for younger children.

Poorer communities offered a single term of two or three months, or even only a few weeks.

IF YOU WERE A BOY...

and if your father was a professional, such as a lawyer or a minister, and if you lived in or near Boston or Cambridge, considered the heart of intellectualism in America, he'd probably want you to enter Harvard College.

As soon as you reached your fourth birthday, your father would drill you in Latin, considered the mark of an educated man. At the age of six or eight, you'd enter the Boston Latin Grammar School where you'd study Ovid, Virgil, Cicero, algebra, geometry, history, elocution and Greek. Your teachers would be of the best caliber, graduates from English colleges or Harvard. About the age of eleven or fourteen, depending on your ability, you'd be eligible to take the Harvard examinations which tested your ability to read classical authors, to speak and write Latin both in prose and verse, and to inflect the paradigms of Greek nouns and verbs. With this knowledge, you'd be ready to become a minister, lawyer, politican or other professional leader.

If your father was a tradesman, he'd probably gear you to earn a living the same way he did. After you learned "the three R's," either at home or in grammar school, you'd be apprenticed to live and work with an experienced tradesman, such as a printer, for several years until you'd be ready to start your own business.

If you were expected to become a farmer, it was felt that the simple rudiments of readin', 'ritin', and 'rithmethic, would serve you well throughout your life. You'd learn how to farm from your father.

If You Were a Girl...

you had no access to Harvard or to any higher education. Colleges were not open to girls.[7]

It was felt that girls, who were to marry and manage families and homes, could do very well without book instruction. In fact, many people felt that knowledge could be injurious to a woman's health.

No one expected you to earn money or have a career.

If you were a girl living in the eighteenth century, you probably were unable to write your name. Less than one woman in a dozen could do that. If you had to sign an important paper such as a deed, you would "make your mark." You would draw an "X" on a line.

The early laws on education did not recognize girls as eligible for school because they stated that "the word 'children' is to be interpreted to mean 'boys.'"[8]

In 1788 in Northampton, Massachusetts, town officials voted that no money would be spent on schooling for girls. In Boston girls were allowed to attend public schools during the summer months only, and only if there were seats left vacant by boys.[9]

In grade school girls were not taught as boys were. You were taught reading, writing, and spelling, but greater attention was paid to sewing, knitting, and polite behavior. You were expected to embroider an elaborate sampler, a square of linen or silk, on which you stitched the alphabet in capitals and small letters, the digits, a verse of sentiment, and your name, age, and home. You included borders, trees, flowers, sometimes animals and people in many colored silks or worsteds.

Girls stopped attending school between the ages of twelve and fourteen, and thereafter stayed home, helping mother with the housework and with younger brothers and sisters.

If your parents were poor and you needed to earn a living, there were only a few occupations open to a "respectable" young woman: housemaid, factory worker, seamstress, laundress, teacher.

IF YOU WERE A PRIVILEGED GIRL...

you took private lessons in French, music, classical literature, dancing, needle point, or some similar subject from a local tutor or college graduate who taught from his or her home.

If your father had money and believed in additional education for girls– you'd be sent to a private boarding school or academy for a year or two. These schools were established to "finish" a girl, to turn her into a woman of accomplishment and grace. Here, you studied French, fancy needlework, dancing, and elegant manners.

No matter how you were tracked educationally, at about the age of fourteen, your parents would begin to prime you for marriage to ensure that you would have a husband, home and family.

BOYS AND GIRLS HAD TO BE "QUIET AS A MOUSE..."

"and as industrious as a beaver." You had to do what the master or schoolmarm expected. If you didn't, you would be punished.

Generally, you'd attend for about eight hours a day, from eight in the morning until four o'clock in the afternoon, sometimes six days a week. Your studies included reading, spelling, writing, grammar, geography, and arithmetic (addition, subtraction, multiplication, division, and a bit on fractions). Algebra, Latin and French were offered only when the teacher could teach those subjects.

Your day started with copying in your best penmanship a page your master had written into your ruled paper copy book. You wrote with a quill pen and prepared your ink with water. Sometimes you copied from your speller, grammar or arithmetic book onto a slate board.

Next you read and reviewed from your spelling book, Bible, or primer which was a reading text with alphabet, syllables, poetry, hymns, stories and moral tales. Primers were published in series, so you began to learn to read with the First Reader and, when you were ready, you went on to the Second Reader and then the Third Reader.

But you were lucky if you had a book. Many schools did not have them and students used whatever text they could find. One person would have a worn volume belonging to a grandfather, for instance. Another would have an older brother's book, and a third would have been able to buy a new book.

About half-past ten you had a short recess, after which the class started a general "spell," with the teacher announcing words from a spelling book for pupils to spell. Sometimes two students would choose sides for a spelling match. This might be followed by recitations of poetry, oratory, and dialogues. Patrick Henry's "Give me liberty or give me death" speech was quite popular.

Your Studies Could be Difficult.

In arithmethic you had to tackle problems concerning discounts, profit and loss, and fractions– problems, for instance, concerning how many leaps imaginary hounds made when they chased imaginary hares for a certain distance.

In grammar you had to analyze, or parse, a sentence.

In geography you were expected to repeat the names of rivers, bays, straits, gulfs and peninsulas.

In the eighteenth century history was not taught at all. In the early nineteenth century educators began to feel that history could cultivate your moral, spiritual, and patriotic attitude of mind. So it was taught in the upper grades for short periods of time. American history was considered sufficient for American youngsters to learn. Generally, you had to learn a succession of dates, names of presidents, etc.

In physiology you had to know the names of bones and muscles.

YOU HAD TO MEMORIZE...

passages which stressed a moral, historical, religious or ethical principle.
For instance, you had to recite some of the speeches of Shakespeare, or
sections from the Latin poet Virgil, or verses from the Bible.

Reciting from memory is called learning by rote. This method promotes
a mechanical process which does not require you to think and reason.
It can be compared to what a parrot does.

WHAT IF YOU COULD NOT COMMIT
YOUR LESSON TO MEMORY?

The teacher might make you sit on a tall stool in the corner of the room all day wearing a pointed dunce hat. Or the teacher might pin a sign on you which read, "Idle Student." It was felt that these punishments ridiculed you so that you would learn your lessons.

If You Misbehaved, You Could Be...

(1) locked in a dark closet,
(2) slapped on your hand with a ferule (ruler),
(3) flogged with a birch rod or a cowhide or a rattan.

One master split the largest end of a tree branch and fitted the split on the culprit's nose. Another drew a circle on the blackboard and made the youngster touch it with his nose for a protracted period of time. Other teachers commanded that you stand behind a door, or copy a sentence, such as "Procrastination is the thief of time," a hundred times.

"The heavy gad."
The common term for five feet
of bendable sapling.

Many boys and girls took beatings at school only to go home to take another from their fathers because it was thought that whippings would turn bad children into good, learned children.

How Different Was Bronson Alcott's School!

His idea was to awaken thought rather than memory.

"If you obtain one thought, you possess more than a person who has $1000," he proclaimed.

Learning, he thought, was a natural process. Nature and life were the means for growth, renewal, and the perfection of spirit. The most important aspect in a person's life was spiritual existence, to be cultivated for the development of mind, heart, and character.

He based his view of education on the work of the Swiss reformer, Pestalozzi,[10] and he called his system, Spiritual Culture.

He tried to lead children to knowledge, intuitively, through a deductive method of dialogue, following the examples of the greatest of teachers, Pythagoras,[11] Socrates,[12] Plato,[13] and Jesus.

The schoolroom, Bronson Alcott thought, was the laboratory where new ideas were to be tested, and each child should find his/her own inner drive to action.

The wood-burning stove, he said, kindled the fire of the mind.

BRONSON ALCOTT WAS A TALL, FAIR, BLUE-EYED, HANDSOME, HARD-WORKING YANKEE.

He was kind, calm, practical, clever. Largely self-educated, he'd read many books and he was a former peddler who'd travelled by foot through many states selling pots and pans and other household wares.

He'd organized conversational excursions, gathering individuals about him who'd pay to converse with him. He was friends with the most intellectual men in our country, including some of our most eminent writers, Ralph Waldo Emerson, Henry David Thoreau, and Nathaniel Hawthorne.

A brilliant young neighbor and teacher, Elizabeth Peabody, believed in Bronson Alcott's unconventional methods and speedily found eighteen five-to-ten year-olds who would enroll. She organized furniture and space "to cultivate the mind and heart," and promised to serve as his assistant.

THERE WERE BOOKS:

Johnson's Dictionary, Pike's Speller, the *Bible, Pilgrim's Progress, Commonplace Book of Poetry,* Quarles' *Emblems,* Northcote's *Fables,* Spencer's *Faery Queen,* the *Iliad, The Ancient Mariner,* Emerson's *Nature,* Homeric hymns, and collections of the famous writers, Shakespeare, Wordsworth, Coleridge, Milton, and Maria Edgeworth.

His curriculum included reading, writing, arithmetic, spelling, parsing, composition, literature, biology, geography, Latin, drawing, music, singing, marching and dancing.

It also included such unusual subjects as defining and illustrating words, writing in journals, studying the human body and its culture, studying readings from works of geniuses, sketching maps, analyzing motives to study, reasonings on conduct– and participating in conversations. (Science was not of primary importance, he thought, because most students were too young for it.)

You Began the Day at the Temple School...

by walking quickly and quietly to your desk which faced the wall and was spaced apart from those on either side so that you and your neighbors did not distract each other.

If you entered the room noisily, the mild but firm Mr. Alcott asked you to re-enter the room in the proper manner, with self-control.

The first hour of school was devoted to copying letters from large tablets placed on each desk. Mr. Alcott walked from one student to another, correcting errors and fixing pens.

Your homework assignment was often writing a journal of mind and conscience. This, he felt, would lead to habits of mental analysis and was vital in growing self-knowledge and self-inspection.

"Gather up the fragments which otherwise would have been lost."

"Give unity to your being."

Play Was as Important as Study.

School should last only about four hours a day, Bronson Alcott thought, because children should spend the rest of the time playing. Boston parents were so aghast at this incredible idea that they threatened to withdraw their children from his school. So he was forced to hold to the longer hours that other schools maintained.

Making and mending goose quill pens consumed much time.

"WRITE DOWN THE PICTURE MADE BY YOUR MIND ON THINGS."

"I hope you will soon write the thoughts and feelings that come up from your soul about these things. These thoughts and feelings are your inward life."

If you whispered, Mr. Alcott might say, "Does the sun make a noise?" Or, "A perfect machine is one which makes the least noise."

If you drummed on your desk with your pen, he would say something like: "Is it all right for each person in a group to act as he or she wishes?"

If you interrupted or laughed out loud: "Do you have the resolution not to interrupt with unnecessary words?"... or "with laughing?"

If you were noisy, Mr. Alcott might say: "With your thoughtlessness you have interfered with my hearing the lesson."

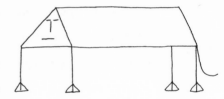

If the entire class was noisy, he stopped. "Why don't I go on? Because we are all making such a noise."

He'd wait patiently, as long as was necessary, until the class brought themselves to order.

After the lesson, he would comment that he was very glad his students had governed themselves.

Fly-leaf scribbles made by nineteenth century students in their school textbooks.

Suppose you were drawing pictures when you were supposed to be listening, Alcott would say, "If you stopped your ears when your mother wanted to say something, how would you know what she was saying?"

AT TEN O'CLOCK...

Mr. Alcott softly asked everyone to move chairs to the center of the room in a semi-circle, making sure that there was space between each chair, so that no one would be distracted by another person.

Opening with his favorite exercise, he asked for spellings, definitions and illustrations of words. Words were signs of thoughts.

On one day "lone" was the first word. "Do you ever feel lonely?" he asked. "When there are people present?... When there are no people present? Loneliness is in the mind, a feeling independent of circumstances."

The word "look" was defined. He asked, "How does the soul look out?" Someone answered: "Through the eyes."

"How does the soul look in?"
"By the thoughts turning round."

"The soul looks in with the eyes as well as out. Is not the soul itself an eye? And what is reflection?"
One student answered, "Reflection seems to imply a looking glass."

Mr. Alcott responded, "It is not the best name for the act of mind I was speaking of; there is a better word for this– thought."

"Meek" was defined. Mr. Alcott described a meek character and asked if there were any meek boys or girls in school, and whether anyone knew anyone who was meek. No one need speak the name aloud, he said. "Let each one think for himself whether he is meek."

If you had a comment, you could raise your hand and speak up.

"What is the meaning of the word brute?"
If you didn't know the answer, you were encouraged to guess.

"What is an oath?"
If your eyes wandered, he waited until they returned.

"What is it to swear? Have any of you ever sworn?"

After discussion, he asked about other words, such as nice, none, pain, beauty. "A word," he'd say, "has saved a life when spoken at the right time."

FEW WERE HIS RULES, FEW HIS PUNISHMENTS.

If you threw a spitball across the room, Mr. Alcott would stop the lesson
and ask, "Are you willing to be punished?"
Would you murmer, "Yes"?

"Is your mother kind when she punishes you?"
  What would be your answer?

"You see how the good in this class have to wait on the bad.
  The good must suffer in the sharing of the evil of the world."

DISCIPLINE WAS A MATTER THAT CONCERNED THE WHOLE GROUP.

"Examine yourself." He appealed to your inner conscience.
"What made you do this?"
  You would have to answer.

"Will you tell the class what you should have done?"
  You would have to correct yourself.

PUNISHMENT WAS USED AS A MEANS TO HELP YOU GAIN SELF-CONTROL.

When you'd misbehaved, he'd ask you, "What did you do to receive this punishment?"

He would expect you to apologize for your misbehavior. "I feel I must correct you rather than to leave you with your faults."

If you spoke out of turn, he'd feel you needed correction and might admonish you to turn your face away from him.

Or he might ask you to rise from your seat, go into a hall or ante-room, and stay there by yourself. Or, he might tell you to walk over to an obedient student and touch him or her so that you'd feel the vibes of perfection.

Or, he might shake a good person so that you'd learn that your wrongdoing had hurt others.

Alcott read stories about people who had to choose what to do in difficult situations and, afterwards, he'd ask if these characters had chosen right actions.

IF MR. ALCOTT COULD NO LONGER REASON WITH YOU...

because you did the unthinkable – started a quarrel or fight in the room– he'd stop you by saying something like this: "I feel I am just and that I have good will toward you, but sometimes I have to hurt your body in order to reach your mind."

He'd ask you to get the ferule (ruler) off his desk.

You'd expect to be struck on your hand with the wooden ferule.

But Mr. Alcott might hit his own hand.

Then he would say, "The greatest pain is felt when you watch others suffer. I have willingly borne pain for you."

How would this make you feel?

HE MIGHT GIVE YOU THE RULER...

and hold out his own hand, and issue the command:

"Hit me!"

Would you strike your teacher's hand?
Boys and girls in Bronson Alcott's classroom hesitated to hit him.

Harshly he repeated: "Strike my hand!"
Would you do what some did—
lightly tap your teacher's hand
with the wooden ruler?

"Don't I deserve more than that? *Harder! Hit harder!*"
Would you hit harder?

One student who struck hard burst into tears.

Then Mr. Alcott said, "Isn't it better to hurt the body than to
let the mind go neglected?"
He waited for an answer. How would you answer?

He said, "I hope you do not think I do not love your body and mind.
I love both, but I love your mind most for it is worth more."

Perhaps he'd ask,

"DO YOU THINK YOU WOULD BE BETTER IF YOU WERE NEVER PUNISHED?"

What would you say?

Perhaps he'd ask, "Why did you come to school?
"Do you want to become better?
"If you want to become better, what should you do?
"Do you wish to be corrected when you do something wrong?

"The bad must express that they want to become better and they must ask for correction."

Mr. Alcott felt that students must set their own standards of behavior. They must analyze those feelings that bring about better action. They must examine their conduct and discriminate between outward and inward natures.

Sometimes Mr. Alcott would make a culprit a "superintendent" of the class for a day, so that he or she would obtain a feeling of just control and an idea of superintending self.

BRONSON ALCOTT'S CONVERSATIONS WITH STUDENTS.

A Conversation would begin with Mr. Alcott saying, "Is anyone going to want anything, within the next hour, before we start?"

If you said you wanted to go ice skating or coasting, Mr. Alcott would say, "Very well, you are excused; however, remember, you have many opportunities to go ice skating– you can go ice skating whenever you want. But never again will you have a chance to have this Conversation with this group in this room."

Probably, you'd realize that you should not go ice skating at this point in time.

If you raised your hand and said you needed to go to the outhouse, Mr. Alcott would say, "Very well, we will all wait until you come back."

Would you hurry because your classmates were waiting for you?

CONVERSATIONS WERE MEANT TO ENCOURAGE QUESTIONS AND DEEP THOUGHTS.

Bronson Alcott talked on such subjects as Aspiration,
Love, Faith, Will, Insight, etc.

When all were ready to listen and to participate, Mr. Alcott opened the session: "If you are interested and if you will try to give me your whole attention, hold up your hands."

Everyone would raise their hands.

"Most of us let our thoughts wander, but let us all try to keep them as steady as possible today and if we can do this, we will have an interesting conversation. The best thoughts do not lie on the surface of our minds. We have to dive under to get at them, like pearl fishers.

"I am going to ask you some questions and prove to you that you are capable of thinking on this subject. You will be teaching yourselves and you will be teaching me.

"I do not know all that I am going to say, for I shall have new thoughts that I never had before. Still less do you know all that you are going to say, for you have not thought so much on the subject as I have. But if we will all think, and all say what we think, we shall teach each other.

"It is my object to make you reason, by giving the terms. I have not sought in these conversations to present my owns view of truth, but to call forth yours, and by so doing make you conscious of your own powers of finding it."

WORDS WERE THE CHIEF SYMBOLS OF SPIRIT.

With the word, your mind could start to work, your feelings quicken, your pulse throb.

"Education, when rightly understood, will be found to lie in the art of asking apt and fit questions, and in thus leading the mind by its own light to the perception of truth."

Bronson Alcott

We know what was said during Alcott's Conversations because his assistants, Elizabeth Peabody, and later Margaret Fuller, recorded them and they were published in books.

Elizabeth Peabody　　　　*Margaret Fuller*

Two Brilliant Teachers

SOME OUTRAGEOUS QUESTIONS

How do you think you
would respond to
Mr. Alcott's
Conversations?

If you want to experience what it was like to participate
in one of Mr. Alcott's Conversations, turn the pages
and answer the questions!

Have you a clear feeling, an idea,
of something, which is not your body,
which you never saw, but which *is* —
which loves, which thinks, which feels?

Do you have proofs that this thing
which is not your body exists?

Have you seen consciousness?

...with your eyes? ...with your ears?

What is your conscience?

Have you looked within yourself
and found your conscience?

When did your conscience begin?

When you were born?

When were you first aware of it?

When you see an infant, you observe
that its little body is full of motion.

It seems to be constantly seeking after something.

Do you think the spirit within it feels
and tries to express its feelings and wants
through the senses?

What makes us good?

Does your conscience make you
do right and wrong?

Do you think your wishes are bad?

Do you think your wishes are good?

Did you ever wish to hit someone
or something?

When you wish to do wrong, what stops you?

What is wisdom?

The spirit feels, judges, uses knowledge.

This is wisdom.

The senses gain knowledge of outward things:
the spirit feels, judges of, disposes,
uses this knowledge, and makes it an instrument,
and this is wisdom, is it not?

Does spirit come through the senses?

Has the mind any other senses than those
which it puts into the body's five senses?

Does wisdom come through the senses?

Do we have other senses
besides the body's senses?

Has the mind a sense about right and wrong?

Can a person who has great knowledge
be bad and unwise?

Do you keep your feelings within the limits
of what your conscience says is right?

Do you live mostly in an inward, or outward world?

Have you an inward, a spiritual sense
of right and wrong?

Can you do wrong and
escape punishment in your mind?

Should you like to be good?

Who is the best person in the world?

Are you what you want to be?

Are you all that you can be?

Conscience is spirit acting on duty.

Mind is spirit thinking.

Heart is spirit loving.

Soul is spirit feeling.

Sense is spirit inquiring into the external world.

Body is the instrument and organ of spirit.

The action of these is divided between
consciousness and conscience.

What have you learned?

Have you been interested in this conversation?

Will you be influenced by this
conversation in the future?

If you wish to compare what you said in this
Conversation with what Mr. Alcott's students said
in 1836, turn the page.

Bronson Alcott's 1836 Conversation

The following is from *Conversations with Children on the Gospels, held in Mr. Alcott's School; unfolding the Doctrine and Discipline of Human Culture,* conducted and edited by Amos Bronson Alcott, Vol. 1 & 2, Boston: James Munroe and Co., 1836, Vol. 2, 1837. Margaret Fuller was Alcott's assistant and recorded this Conversation, as well as many others. The ages of the children ranged from six to twelve. All were from prominent families in Boston whose sectarian affiliations were Universalist, Unitarian, Baptist, Episcopalian, Methodist, Swedenborgian, and Free Enquirer.

CONVERSATION I

Idea of Spirit

Evidence of Consciousness

Alcott.　Have you a clear feeling, idea, of something, which is not your body, which you never saw, but which is– which loves, which thinks, which feels? (All gradually held up their hands) Now what are your proofs? (Many hands fell.) Those who have proofs may answer in turn.

Lemuel.　I am sure of it, but I do not know why.

Alexander.　I have heard you say so.

Alcott.　You have trusted to me? Well! that is faith in testimony.

William C.　I cannot prove it, but I feel it.

Alcott.　You and Lemuel have the evidence of consciousness. You cannot think otherwise.

George K.　I thought of my mind as my proof.

Andrew.　I thought of my conscience; when I do right I feel that I have one.

William B.　I thought and I felt. That is Spirit.

Charles.　I felt your question working within me, and that was my proof.

Edward B.　Conscience is my proof. I feel when I do right and wrong, and that is my soul.

Lucy.   I have proof, but I cannot express it.

Emma.   I knew before I was asked.

Alcott.   It is a sentiment with you and Lucy.

Josiah.   Self-government.

Edward J.   Conscience.

(Some other answers were repetitious.)

Alcott.   So you all think there is something, which is not body. But have you seen it; who has seen conscience? (All made the negative sign.) Then your eyes, it seems, did not tell you of this being, which is not body. (All shook their heads.) Nor your ears?

George K.   I have heard my father and mother talk about conscience with my ears, and so I believed it was.

Alcott.   What believed? your ears? or was it the conscience within you that understood what your father and mother meant by conscience?

George K.   Yes, that was the way. But our ears do a little good.

Alcott.   Yes, the spirit uses the organs of sense, though it is something else than these organs.

Edward B.   It only seems as if our senses themselves saw, and heard, and smelled; but it is the mind which is really doing those things with the eyes and ears for its instruments.

Alcott.   Now in all this, what are your senses after? What is it, that this something within you wants, when it uses your eyes, ears, and other organs of sense; what does it go out after?

John D.   When we use our tongue, the spirit goes after our food.

Lemuel.   When we look, it wants something to see; and when we listen, it wants something to hear; and when we taste, it wants something to eat and drink.

Alexander. When we look, the spirit comes to help.

Welles. When we hear, the spirit is after instruction.

Charles. The senses are a kind of feelers, to show forth what the spirit within wants.

Alcott. When you see an infant, you observe that its little body is full of motion. It seems to be constantly seeking after something. Do you think the spirit within it feels, and tries to express its feelings and wants through the senses?

(Charles assented.)

Emma. The spirit goes out through the senses after outward things.

Alcott. After what outward things? (Emma did not answer)

Mr. Alcott. Josiah, what is your answer?

Josiah. My mind sees through my eyes.

Edward J. The spirit comes out to see and hear.

Hales. My mind sees with my eyes.

Joseph. The senses are to help keep the mind good and the body good.

Alcott. Do they always keep all good?

Joseph. When we let them.

Alcott. What hinders them sometimes?

Joseph. Anger.

Alcott. What lets them make us good at other times?

Joseph. Love.

John D. When a baby goes into his mind to feel, he feels after wisdom and goodness.

Alcott. The infant goes inward, then, for wisdom and goodness, and outward for food for the body, and for knowledge?

Andrew.	When we have done right, the spirit comes out in our eyes; and when we have done wrong, it comes out and makes us ashamed to show our face.
William B.	The senses are made so that your spirit, and soul, and mind, may get knowledge and be kept alive; for if you had no senses you could not be very wise; and you need the senses to communicate to others, what you gain from the use of your senses.
Alcott.	Where does life come from, William?
William B.	From the spirit.
Alcott.	Your answer implies that life comes from without, through the senses; for you speak of the spirit's being kept alive by them, as if there was something that came from objects of sense to keep it alive.
William B.	Oh, I do not mean that; I mean that one person, by means of the senses, is able to keep alive the spirit of others.
Edward B.	I think the spirit goes into the eyes, ears, etc., after knowledge. But I think the soul would have some wisdom, even if we had no senses at all, – were blind, deaf, and all.
William B.	I think people who had no senses might be good, but could not be very wise.
Alcott.	What is wisdom? (A pause.) Does not wisdom stand for all that the spirit gets from itself? The senses gain knowledge of outward things; the spirit feels, judges of, disposes, uses, this knowledge, and makes it an instrument, and this is wisdom, is it not? Is not this the distinction?
Edward B.	A person who has great knowledge has greater means, sometimes, of being bad and unwise.
Alcott.	Do you remember the two trees in Paradise? the tree of knowledge and the tree of life – of wisdom perhaps?
Lucy.	We ought to have some senses to tell us when we do right, and how.

Lucia.   There are senses in the spirit for that!

Alcott.   What other senses have we but the body's senses; what are the names of the spirit's senses?

George K.   The mind has senses, which it puts into the body's senses.

Alcott.   Has the mind any other senses than those which it puts into the body's five senses?

George K.   Yes; a sense of good.

Mr. Alcott.   Has the mind a sense about right and wrong?

Several.   Yes; conscience.

Mr. Alcott.   How many of you have this inward, this spiritual sense of right and wrong? (A pause.) Yesterday one of the boys behaved wrong and was punished. When he came into school, yesterday morning, his eyes looked large and bright. When he comes into school today, his eyes are half shut; why is this?

Several.   Conscience.

The Rest.   The spirit's sense.

Welles.   Shame is one of the spirit's senses.

Mr. Alcott.   The boy I have been speaking of may rise and show himself. (Several rise.) Well! I thought of one; but conscience, it seems has thought of many more.

Lucy and others exclaimed. The spirit's senses.

Alcott.   Such of you then, as think there is something within you which is no part of your body, but which moves your body, acts in it, and is better than your body, and your body lives upon it, may hold up your hands. (All held up hands.) How many think a good name for this is mind? (Several held up hands.) Or soul, or God, or intellect, or conscience, or spirit?

(Most agreed upon God as the best name. One said Spirit was the best; another said God and Spirit were the same.)

Alcott.   I prefer the word *Spirit*. And soon we shall begin to talk of a particular Spirit that came into the world and took a body; and acted in the world; and we shall inquire what became of it when it left the world. What Spirit are we going to talk about?

All.   Jesus Christ.

Alcott.   How many of you will always know hereafter what I mean by the word *spirit*, when I use it?

(All held up their hands.)

Andrew.   I think the word conscience would be a better word than spirit.

Alcott.   *Conscience* is spirit acting on duty; *Mind* is spirit thinking; *Heart* is spirit loving; *Soul* is spirit feeling; *Sense* is spirit inquiring into the external world; *Body* is the instrument and organ of spirit. The action of these is divided between consciousness and conscience.

MISCELLANY

A BIOGRAPHICAL AFTERWORD

Amos Bronson Alcott was a teacher/philosopher admitted into the intellectual circle of ministers known as Transcendentalists during the 1830s-40s. The other non-clerics were Henry David Thoreau and Margaret Fuller, who was the only woman who played a vital role in this group for a protracted period of time.

Transcendentalism was a reaction against the rigid Calvinism and Unitarianism of the day. It can be defined as truth, beauty, individualism, the harmony of nature, and the divinity of humankind. The major spokesman of Transcendentalism, Ralph Waldo Emerson, proclaimed in direct oppostion to Calvinism that good was within every person and that every person could mediate directly with God. The leading advocates included William Ellery Channing, George Ripley, Theodore Parker as well as Alcott, Thoreau, and Fuller. All were radicals who were regarded as outrageous and rebellious, though none resorted to violence or picketing. The spoken and the written word – voice and quill pen – were their sole weapons.

Because Bronson Alcott's writings were often vague and abstract to the point of diffusion, he was often ridiculed, and because he could not earn enough money to provide a decent living for his wife and five daughters, he has often been denigrated. But he was a kind, tender, gentle man who practiced innovative teaching methods. He was the father of Louisa May Alcott, who became the successful author of *Little Women* and other books for young people, and who later described her father's educational process in her sequel, *Little Men*.

With the birth of his children, Bronson Alcott recorded his infants' growth in a book entitled, *History of an Infant: Observations on the Phenomena of Life as Developed in the Progressive History of an Infant During the First Year of its Existence.* No one had as yet delineated this subject in detail. He insisted on watching his third child's birth, an act considered at that time totally uncouth.

The controversy that was the eventual ruination of The Temple School started after Alcott decided to publish books describing his educational methods which he called Spirit Soul or Spiritual Culturalism. Elizabeth Peabody had taken classroom notes which were printed verbatim in *Record of A School*. Children's psyches, their mental and physical growth had never before been considered, and authorities were attracted to his unique ideas, visited and observed his school, and Alcott began to experience an increase in enrollment.

With almost forty students, Alcott opened the second year with a new series of conversations. He again instructed Elizabeth Peabody to take notes. Dissension developed. She felt he elicited thoughts from the children which were essentially his own thoughts. When she offered criticism or made suggestions, he turned a deaf ear.

Alcott began his second school year by talking about the life of Jesus and the meaning of the spirit within each person, and then he started reading from the Bible on the births of John the Baptist and Jesus. He asked leading questions and used such words and phrases as "conceived," "deliver," "seed," "flesh," "circumcision," "conjugal relations," "mothers have signs," "she gives up her body to God, and he works upon it," "the seed of a human being is placed in the midst of matter which nourishes it."

His mild lessons may have been the first on sex education, but it was an age when adults told youngsters that babies came from angels.

Peabody had missed these fateful sessions, but had arranged as substitute-recorder her sister, Sophia, who admired Alcott and took down his words exactly as he delivered them. She didn't know these notes were to be published.

Elizabeth Peabody suggested that Alcott "black pencil" the manuscript, but he refused. Then she insisted on writing a foreword to the book, stating that though Alcott's teaching was superlative, she herself was opposed to some of his ideas. Then she resigned.

About this time Ralph Waldo Emerson had met twenty-six year-old Margaret Fuller who was looking for a teaching job in order to help support her mother and five younger siblings. Thus, at The Temple School "Miss Fuller" taught literature, Latin, French and German and was instructed to record Alcott's Conversations.

Public bombardment against Alcott climaxed as copies of *Conversation with the Children on the Gospels* were being snatched up. A hundred sold within four days.

Clergymen called the book "filthy." A writer in a major newspaper, the *Courier,* suggested that Mr. Alcott be prosecuted for blasphemy. Alcott was labelled insane, half-witted, an ignorant charlatan. The most revered sage in Harvard and Boston circles, Andrews Norton, claimed that one third of the book was absurd, one third was blasphemous, and one third was obscene.

Emerson explained Alcott's methods in a letter to the *Courier.* Another friend, James Freeman Clarke, wrote publicly that Alcott was another Socrates. Fuller defended Alcott in various letters, and Elizabeth Peabody published another defense but it was ignored.

Student enrollment at The Temple School dropped to ten.

When the book on which Margaret Fuller worked, *Conversations II*, was published, it was not really read by anyone.

Instead of paying her, Alcott praised Fuller to another educator who was starting a similar school in Providence, Rhode Island, and Fuller left the Boston area to teach there.

Alcott struggled on with his school, but when he admitted a negro child, his enrollment dropped to four, the negro and his own three daughters.

Thus, in 1839 Alcott joined the ranks of the unemployed, picking up part-time work digging and hammering for farmers. Over the next few years he wrote articles which were printed in the Transcendentalist magazine, *The Dial*, edited by Margaret Fuller and for a time published by Elizabeth Peabody. The public ridiculed and parodied his writings. As years passed, remainders of his books were sold as wastepaper.

In 1842 two radical English reformers, Charles Lane and Henry G. Wright opened a school in Ham, Surrey, naming it Alcott House after Alcott's innovative methods. Thanks to Ralph Waldo Emerson who donated funds from one of his lectures, Alcott was able to visit.

In 1843 Alcott started his own utopia, Fruitlands, with Lane and Wright who had crossed the ocean to the United States. Fruitlands boasted ten apple trees and ninety acres of rolling hills and streams outside of Harvard, Massachusetts.* Here, the idealists believed that chickens had "the same right to life as human babies," therefore chickens were not to be eaten, and "the cow should not be robbed of her milk," therefore cows were not to be milked. Alcott's wife, Abby, had to fight for her baby's right to drink milk.

The communal family insisted on plain housing, vegetarian diet, linen clothing (because cotton came from slave labor), "pure bathing, unsullied dwellings, open conduct, gentle behavior, kindly sympathies, serene minds." About fifteen men eventually joined, all of whom used hand spades in the fields instead of beasts of burden and insisted on growing only those vegetables that grew toward heaven, such as corn. Carrots and potatoes were vetoed because their roots grew downward.

A woman who showed up to help asked Abby if there were any beasts of burden on the place. Abby replied: "Only one woman." In time, the Fruitlanders succumbed to putting an ox to work, and eventually they agreed that potatoes were acceptable for eating.

Fruitlands lasted only a few months because Alcott, Lane, and Wright decided to go off on an East Coast lecture tour just when it was time to bring in the harvest. Also, Lane left because Alcott and wife would not live up to standards of total sexual abstinence. Lane claimed marriage obstructed a wider humanity. He and son (from an early marriage) joined the Shakers, the nearby community wherein sexes were separated and intercourse was ruled out. In 1846 Lane returned to England, converted to Catholicism, married, and had five children.

* Fruitlands, restored today, is immensely rewarding to visit.

In 1850 Abby Alcott, in order to earn money since husband didn't, operated an employment agency out of her house in Boston. She placed poor immigrants into wealthy homes as servants. She became Boston's first social worker by finding wealthy patrons who paid her salary while she surveyed the needs of the poor and made recommendations for education and job training. As a young woman Louisa May Alcott took it upon herself to earn enough money by sewing and teaching to support the family, and eventually became one of the country's most successful authors.

In 1861 Elizabeth Peabody founded the first American kindergarten, based on the theories of the German educator, Frederic Froebel, whose methods she observed first hand when she visited Germany in 1867.[14] Mary, her sister who was married to Horace Mann, founder of Antioch College, worked with her. Elizabeth advocated that kindergartens be established for the poor, lectured on teacher training, and published articles and books as well as the magazine, *Kindergarten Messenger*, and started the Froebel Union in the United States. In 1870 she opened the first free public kindergarten.

From 1859-1865 as the concerns of Transcendentalism slipped into the battle of emancipation, Bronson Alcott was at last acknowledged and listened to, at least in Concord, Massachusetts, for his best capabilities, elegant conversation and moral integrity. The elders appointed him superintendent of schools. In this capacity, the silver-haired sage walked from school to school to interview teachers and hold classes. He introduced the production of school festivals, and wrote annual reports which received wide circulation.

In 1879 Louisa May Alcott established one of her father's dreams, The Concord School of Philosophy, an informal summer school which he operated on the grounds of their home, Orchard House.* Here he organized sessions and speakers which furthered Transcendentalist ideas.

Always considered an impractical dreamer— and to give close study to his life is to find him eccentric and flawed— Bronson Alcott has never been recognized as a groundbreaker who helped to bring child psychology and inductive teaching into modern educational methods. Leading educators who came later in the century seem not to have realized that their "new" theories had earlier been practiced in the Temple School. Reconsidered, Alcott can be evaluated as a forerunner of one of our country's most influential educators who struggled for the cause of free inquiry and the betterment of humankind— John Dewey.[15]

---

*Orchard House and the Concord School of Philosophy stand open to tourists today in Concord, Massachusetts.

QUARTER CARD OF DISCIPLINE AND STUDIES IN MR. ALCOTT'S SCHOOL FOR THE SPRING TERM CURRENT 1836.

THE TUITION AND DISCIPLINE ARE ADDRESSED IN DUE PROPORTION TO THE THREEFOLD NATURE OF CHILDHOOD.

THE SPIRITUAL FACULTY.	THE IMAGINATIVE FACULTY.	THE RATIONAL FACULTY.
MEANS OF ITS DIRECT CULTURE.	MEANS OF ITS DIRECT CULTURE.	MEANS OF ITS DIRECT CULTURE.
1. Listening to Sacred Readings.	1. Spelling and Reading.	1. Defining Words.
2. Conversations on the GOSPELS.	2. Writing and Sketching from Nature.	2. Analysing Speech.
3. Writing Journals.	3. Picturesque Geography.	3. Self-Analysis.
4. Self-Analysis and Self Discipline.	4. Writing Journals and Epistles.	4. Arithmetic.
5. Listening to Readings from Works of Genius.	5. Illustrating Words.	5. Study of the HUMAN BODY.
6. Motives to Study and Action.	6. Listening to Readings.	6. Reasonings on Conduct.
7. Government of the School.	7. Conversations.	7. Discipline.

The Subjects of Study and Means of Discipline are disposed through the Week in the following general Order.

TIME	SUNDAY	MONDAY	TUESDAY	WEDNESDAY	THURSDAY	FRIDAY	SATURDAY
IX	Sacred READINGS with Conversations.	STUDYING Spelling & Defining and Writing in Journals.	STUDYING Geography and Sketching Maps in Journals.	STUDYING THE GOSPEL and Writing in Journals.	STUDYING Parsing Lesson and Writing in Journals.	PARAPHRASING Text of Readings and Writing in Journals.	COMPLETING Account of Week's Studies in Journals.
X	Listening to Services at CHURCH and	SPELLING with Illustrative Conversations on the Meaning & Use of Words.	RECITATIONS in Geography with Picturesque Readings and Conversations.	READINGS and Conversations on SPIRIT as displayed in the Life of CHRIST.	ANALYSING Speech Written and Vocal on Tablets with Illustrative Conversations.	READINGS with Illustrative Conversations on the Sense of the Text.	READINGS from Works of Genius with Applications and Conversations.
XI	Reading BOOKS from School Library or others at Home.	STUDYING Arithmetic with Demonstrations in Journals.	DRAWING FROM NATURE in Journals with Mr. Graeter.	CONVERSATIONS on the HUMAN BODY and its Culture.	COMPOSING and Writing Epistles in Journals.	STUDYING Arithmetic with Demonstrations in Journals.	REVIEW of Journals Week's Conduct and Studies.
XII / I	*RECREATION ON THE COMMON OR IN THE ANTE-ROOM.*						
	INTERMISSION FOR REFRESHMENT AND RECREATION.						
III		STUDYING Latin and Writing in Journals.	STUDYING Latin with Recitations.	RECREATIONS and Duties At Home.	STUDYING Latin with Recitations.	STUDYING Latin and Writing in Journals.	RECREATIONS and Duties At Home.
IV		STUDYING Latin and Writing in Journals.	STUDYING Latin with Recitations.	RECREATIONS and Duties At Home.	STUDYING Latin with Recitations.	STUDYING Latin and Writing in Journals.	RECREATIONS and Duties At Home.

CHRONOLOGY

1799 Birth of Bronson Alcott.

1834 Opening in September of Bronson Alcott's Masonic Temple School in Boston, Mass. with Elizabeth Peabody serving as Alcott's assistant.

1835 Publication of *Record of a School*, a description of Alcott's methods and conversations, recorded by Elizabeth Peabody.

1836 Peabody resigned as teacher at Alcott's Temple School in August, and in December Margaret Fuller took over the position, teaching literature, Latin, French, German, and she began to record Alcott's Conversations for a new volume to be entitled *Conversations II*. During this same month *Conversations with Children on the Gospels*, a record of Alcott's Conversations recorded by Elizabeth Peabody, was published. The book was publicly denounced. Clergymen called the book "filthy." Alcott was labelled insane, half-witted, an ignorant charlatan.

1837 *Conversations II* was published in February. In the spring Margaret Fuller resigned from The Temple School and took a position with The Greene Street School in Providence, Rhode Island. Alcott was forced to auction off school furniture and many books. His enrollment dropped to ten, and he moved his school to a small boxlike room in the basement of the Masonic Hall.

1838 Bronson Alcott moved his school out of the Masonic Temple into his home. He had about twenty pupils.

1839 Bronson Alcott enrolled a negro girl in the Temple School in June. Within a few weeks the parents of his students sent a representative to ask him to dismiss the child, but he refused. Therefore, all children except one were withdrawn from Alcott's school, and he was forced to close.

1850 Death of Margaret Fuller.

1859-65 Bronson Alcott served as superintendent of schools in Concord, Massachusetts.

1860 Elizabeth Peabody founded the first kindergarten in America, and ten years later established the first free public kindergarten in the United States. Constantly encouraging teacher training, she spent her final years travelling and lecturing on education.

1879 Louisa May Alcott established The Concord School of Philosphy for her father, on the grounds of their home, Orchard House.

1888 Deaths of Bronson Alcott and Louisa May Alcott.

1894 Death of Elizabeth Peabody.

CREATIVE SUGGESTIONS FOR ADULTS USING THIS BOOK WITH CHILDREN

When I first read Alcott's Conversations, I could hardly believe that children could answer profound questions in the intelligent manner recorded by Margaret Fuller and Elizabeth Peabody. Yet, in workshops I found that children can and do have deep thoughts and can express them. One thing is certain, they won't answer questions if they are not asked!

Conduct your own Conversation with children, using the questions in this book as a guide– the children will surprise you with their responses! Or let them read the questions to themselves and answer them silently. If they don't answer, it probably does not matter. Perhaps they need time to digest a question. Perhaps tomorrow they will find an answer. Perhaps their answer will change in the next hour, or in the next year. That the questions are posed is what is important.

Probably it is easiest to have a conversation with a group of children of various ages. This is because one child will inspire the next; sharing of ideas will occur.

Before the session, you might find it best to write each step of the process on an index card to which you can easily refer. Then you will be able to move forward in a logical progression and be able to offer details and to quote Alcott accurately. You can practice a bit with the cards before you conduct the Conversation so that you need only glance at the cards while you relate to your audience.

I opened my workshops by introducing myself as Margaret Fuller, a teacher in Bronson Alcott's school. Any teacher/leader can utilize this same idea– dressing and fixing hair or wearing a wig as though you were nineteenth century Fuller, Elizabeth Peabody, or Bronson Alcott. This immediately commands attention and helps you to establish control over the group during the session. You can say you taught in Bronson Alcott's Temple School, which was very different from most schools. Children's imaginations are high– they will go right along with this idea, will realize that you are pretending, and they will love you for doing it.

If you don't know your children by name, you can make sure before the session starts that everyone has a name tag. This will make it easy when you call on individuals, and it will lend intimacy to the group. If you can't use name tags and your group is relatively small, you can spend a few minutes having everyone introduce themselves, giving age and grade in school. This is especially important if the children don't know each other. Right away they will feel more comfortable and will realize that this is a session in which they are encouraged to speak up. Sometimes I ask who are brothers and sisters. Who are relatives? Who are best friends? Etc. It is best if you peg the various relationships and can remember some of the names.

You can lead off with a simple question: What was it like to go to school 150 years ago? If some respond to this intriguing question, so much the better. Listen to comments, one by one. Keep control by having each person raise a hand when he or she wants to comment. Acknowledge each remark, and agree or disagree with whatever is said. If someone says something that is incorrect, softly set the record straight without making him or her feel foolish or guilty. Your goal is to keep the spirit and atmosphere open to expression.

Tell the group about Bronson Alcott, how he loved children, as described in this book. Tell them that most people in the nineteenth century thought children were sinful, but Bronson Alcott believed there was good in each child, that each child had genius within. Say that his ideas of education were different from the typical views of the day.

Talk about one-room schoolhouses and what and how teachers taught, as described in this book. Outline the educational tracking for boys, for girls, for African-Americans, for the poor, for the wealthy, as described in this book. Then ask what would happen in most schools if children misbehaved. Probably one child– or more– will come up with the answer. Every child will relate to the subject of punishment. You can add to their comments, describing other punishments mentioned in this book.

Then focus on how a day at Alcott's school opened, as described in this book. Hold forth on his ideas about journal writing, about recreation, about length of the school day. Keep the dialogue on the subject of schooling; if someone attempts to draw group attention away, say something like, "But we're talking about schools...." "Remember we're in the nineteenth century...."

Next, have the children arrange their chairs in a circle, if possible, with space between each chair so there will be no distractions. (If this is impossible you can describe Alcott's intention.) Then, start the definitions of words and spellings, as described in this book, using the same words, "brute," "lone," meek," asking the children to define and spell them.

You can have the children act out scenarios. "If you whispered...." Choose one child to whisper to another, and you act out what Alcott would have said to the children, as described in this book. "If you were noisy....." Etc. Finally, "if someone threw a spitwad...." You can choose someone to throw a spitwad at someone else, and then you reprimand: "Are you willing to be punished?" Act out the scene; hit the child on the hand with a wooden ruler– lightly, for you are play-acting. If the child shows indignation or psychological hurt at your actually hitting him, you can affirm that this is only play-acting, pretend-like, in order to show how it was done in the nineteenth century. (It is best if you choose the more fun-loving, out-going type of youngsters for these demonstrations.)

Next, stage a fight between two youngsters– of course, you must stop it exactly as Mr. Alcott stopped it, as described in this book, and you must call the "culprit" to the front of the room. You must ask him to hold out his hand. Then you give him the ruler and ask him to hit you, exactly as described in this book, and you follow-up with Alcott's remarks.

By this time the children will be responding eagerly, fascinated with this unusual school, and you are set for the Conversation. Open it with Alcott's words: "If you are interested and if you will try to give me your whole attention, hold up your hands." Etc.

Having Alcott's words and the questions written on index cards will help you greatly.

Let the children's answers come forth spontaneously. Do not insert your opinions; let the children offer their opinions. If you feel an opposing perspective needs to be made, say, "Does everyone think the same as Johnny does?... Does anyone have another idea?" Hopefully, you will pull the other viewpoint from someone else. If not, you might move on to the next question. If you think it's something that needs expression, you might say, "Some people think..." etc.

The trick is to call on those children who have not spoken, yet at the same time to be sensitive to those who prefer to remain silent; thereby you do not pressure or embarrass them. Try to calm the boisterous, and to give time to the quiet. If five of the brightest keep giving all the answers, it's okay, though you need to keep encouraging others to speak out.

At the end of the Conversation, look at your watch and say, "Time for recess!"

RELATED ACTIVITIES

1. Locate a one-room schoolhouse in a nearby area and visit it. Conduct a traditional lesson in it, as was conducted in the nineteenth century. Perhaps have a Bronson Alcott Conversation in it.

2. Invite a person or persons who attended or taught in a one-room schoolhouse to speak to your class. Prepare questions to ask.

3. Talk to a grandmother, aunt, or other adult who has attended or taught in a one-room school. Record the oral history with written word, cassette tape, or video tape. Share with classmates, or with another grade level or with friends.

4. Write an original story or poem or play that revolves around students, teachers and one-room schoolhouses. Read it aloud to classmates, and/or share with another grade level or with friends. Stage the play for an organization or special event. Video tape your experience.

5. Draw a banner or poster of one-room schools, teachers, students, or of Bronson Alcott's Temple School. Show and compare traditional disciplines as opposed to Alcott's innovative methods. Display it in your classroom and/or send it around to every grade to hang in their room for a specified period of time.

6. Video tape a Bronson Alcott Conversation and show it to another grade level or to friends.

7. Make up a series of questions for your own original conversation on a subject of your choice and conduct it with a group of friends or adults.

8. Collect and xerox pictures, stories, and quotes of one-room schoolhouses and make a scrapbook. Locate one-room schoolhouses that have been turned into museums and list them.

9. Find a McGuffey's Reader and/or other textbooks of the nineteenth century, read parts to your class or friends, and explain how they are different from textbooks used today.

10. Write a letter with a quill pen.

11. Choose a nineteenth century person who could not go to school and tell his or her life story in pantomime, dance, or music.

12. Research one or more famous persons who attended one-room schools and write up their stories, emphasizing how they turned opportunities into success.

13. Read about the childhoods of Bronson Alcott, Elizabeth Peabody, and/or Margaret Fuller. Tell their stories to your class, or to another grade level, or your friends.

14. Find out how Elizabeth Peabody started the first kindergarten in America and write a story about it, or tell the story to your class.

15. Color the illustrations in this book.

PHOTO LEGACY OF
AMERICA'S ONE-ROOM SCHOOLHOUSES

District School House No.7 has survived the hazards of almost two centuries. Originally located in the farming community of Candia, New Hampshire, it was built about 1800 with typical post and frame construction. When the Candia Improvement Club presented it to Old Sturbridge Village, Massachusetts, in 1955, careful drawings were made and each timber and board was marked as it was dismantled. Stored in one of the Village's barns on low ground, six months later, a flood lifted the barn from its foundations but the surrounding trees and the weight of the lumber stopped it from floating downstream to destruction. The hardware on the front door is original as are the desks which are carved with initials. Courtesy of Old Sturbridge Village, photos by Henry E. Peach.

District #6 School House originally located at the "Head of Cow Neck" near Manhasset, New York, now stands at Old Bethpage Village Restoration on Long Island, New York. Built in 1826, its restored plaster walls and wainscoting cover the original hand-hewn frame. The building is furnished with functional wooden desks and a wood-burning store. Courtesy of Nassau County. (Originally designated District No. 7 by Town of Hempstead, redesignated No. 6 in 1815).

Mamie McCorkindale Little School Museum in Wayne, Nebraska, refurbished to depict the year 1910. It was named for the supervisor of rural school teacher training at Wayne State College, who taught from 1920 to 1949. The schoolhouse was built in 1880 and served as District 13 for nearly 80 years. Purchased by Wayne State Foundation, and dedicated in 1966, it was moved to the Wayne State College campus and is opened for special occasions.

Laurie James, costumed as Margaret Fuller, leading a workshop in the Mamie McCorkindale Little School Museum.

Photo by LaVon Anderson, Wayne Herald, July 20, 1992.

Bommer Schoolhouse #123 in Marysville, Kansas. Originally white, today it is painted red in commemoration of all little red school houses. It was built in 1885 for a cost of $488, and was named after Henry Bommer, a German immigrant. It operated until 1965. The next year the Marysville Rotary Club purchased it and moved it in 1967 to the city park where it is open to visitors.

The Daise school house being moved to a permanent location in Goodland, Kansas where it was renovated as a museum. Photos by Tina Goodwin, Goodland Daily News, June 24, 1992.

"Snap The Whip," by Winslow Homer, 1872. Oil on canvas. Courtesy of The Butler Institute of American Art, Youngstown, Ohio.

"The Noon Recess," by Winslow Homer, 1873. Wood engraving. Courtesy of the Hood Musem of Art, Dartmouth College, Hanover, New Hampshire; purchased through the Appleton Fund.

Students gather nostalgicly in front of the second oldest surviving one-room school in Maine. The Center School in Alna operated 133 years. Built in 1795, the octagonal bell tower was added during the 1820s, and it was closed in 1962. Today it still stands on the original site and is open to the public as a museum every summer. Photo by Vic Durgin.

FOOTNOTES

1   Margaret Fuller (1810-1850), teacher in Alcott's Temple School in 1836-7, became first American to write a book on equality for women, first editor of *The Dial Magazine*, first woman to conduct paid "Conversations" among the prominent women in Boston, first women journalist on Horace Greeley's *New York Daily Tribune*, first woman foreign correspondent and war correspondent, first woman to step foot inside Harvard Labrary.

2   Elizabeth Peabody (1804-1894), teacher, editor, publisher, initiator of the American kindergarten. She preserved Alcott's system of teaching in her book, *Record of a School*, and published Dr. William Ellery Channing's influential essay on emancipation, *Slavery*, Hawthorne's *Grandfather's Chair, Famous Old People, Liberty Tree*. She was also publisher of *The Dial Magazine* for a limited time. Her writings include *Reminiscences of William Ellery Channing*. She founded the magazines, *Aesthetic Papers*, and *Kindergarten Messenger*, and opened the West Street Bookstore where she was the first to import foreign books and journals and where Margaret Fuller gave her Conversations.

3   Massachusetts had a compulsory attendance law in 1852, requiring school attendance for children between the ages of eight and fourteen, for twelve weeks a year, though it was never enforced.

4   Child labor laws became to appear in 1876. Mild and full of loopholes, they contained statements that children under the age of fifteen could not work more than ten hours a day without parental consent. Many children worked up to sixteen hours per day because parents gave their consent.

5   After the Civil War, some negro children went to separate schools.

6   From town to town there were vast differences in educational quality because monies were often distributed according to the number of families and children in the district.

7   In 1821 Emma Willard opened the Troy Female Seminary in Troy, NY. The first women's colleges opened in the 1830's: Oberlin, Mt. Holyoke, Ipswich Female Seminary, Bradford Academy, Abbot Female Academy in Andover, Wheaton Female Seminary and Maplewood Institute in Pittsfield, MA. Willard believed in the study of higher mathematics, and in 1829, the first public examination of a girl in geometry, caused a public outcry and storm of ridicule. In 1845, Willard promoted women as superintendents of public schools. By 1876 there were 50 normal (teacher training) schools open in the USA.

8 *Old Time Schools and School Books*, page 138.

9 Ibid.

10 Johann Heinrich Pestalozzi (1746-1827), born in Zurich, believed that society could be regenerated through education and that children had individualism and goodness within that could be developed. Children's individuality was sacred. His ideas on discipline were based on love and understanding. One of his followers was Friedrich Froebel. (*See footnote 14.*)

11 Pythagoras, Greek sage of 6th century B.C., who founded a religious-ethical society which fostered bonds of friendship, ritual, symbolism, and rigorous self-control.

12 Socrates (470-399 B.C.), Greek philosopher who introduced a method of discussion, dialogue, and questioning. He gathered bright young men around him, and stimulated logic and inductive cross-examination in order to discover truth and gain knowledge.

13 Plato (428-348/347 B.C.), Greek Philospher who believed that learning could be achieved through discussion and shared inquiry. He was a young associate of Socrates in the last ten years of his life and recorded the work of Socrates in dialogue form.

14 Frederic Froebel (1782-1852), German educator who founded the kindergarten system. His theory of education encompassed the importance of play and a natural "inner unfolding" of the child through spontaneous "self-acitivity." He advocated that the teacher encourage the child's self-development.

15 John Dewey (1859-1952), American philosopher and educational reformer rejected traditional methods of teaching by rote, and who emphasized learning through experpiment and practice. His contribution to the progressive school of education has been acknowledged throughout the world.

BIBLIOGRAPHY

Alcott, Amos Bronson, *Conversations with Children on the Gospels,* held in Mr. Alcott's School; unfolding the Doctrine and Discipline of Human Culture, conducted and edited by Amos Bronson Alcott, Vol. 1 & 2. Boston: James Munroe and Co., 1836, Vol. 2, 1837.

Betts, George Herbert, and Hall, Otis Earle, *Better Rural Schools.* Indianapolis: The Bobbs-Merrill Company, 1914.

Bourgeault, Cynthia, "Kudos for Mr. T.," *Down East Magazine*, April 1993, pp. 28-34, 49-50.

James, Laurie, *Men, Women, and Margaret Fuller.* New York: Golden Heritage Press, 1990.

Johnson, Clifton, *Old-Time Schools and School Books.* New York: The MacMillan Company, 1917.

Johnson, Henry, *Teaching of History in Elementary and Secondary Schools.* New York: The MacMillan Company, 1921.

Loeper, John J., *Going to School in 1776.* New York: Atheneum, 1973.

Loeper, John J., *Going to School in 1876.* New York: Atheneum, 1984.

Peabody, Elizabeth, *Record of a School.* Boston, 1836. Reprinted by Arno Press, 1969.

Roberts, Josephine E., "Elizabeth Peabody and the Temple School." *New England Quarterly,* 15, September 1942, pp. 497-508.

Shepard, Odel, *Pedlar's Progress.* Boston: Little Brown & Co., 1937.

Order Form

Order through your bookstore, distributor or
Mail your check to:

Golden Heritage Press, Inc.
Suite 25D
500 West 43rd Street
New York, NY 10036

Copies:

The Wit and Wisdom of Margaret Fuller
_____ at $8.50 each .... total _____

Why Margaret Fuller Ossoli is Forgotten
_____ at $8.50 each .... total _____

Men, Women, and Margaret Fuller
_____ at $19.95 each .... total _____

Outrageous Questions
_____ at $10.95 (paperback) each .... total _____
_____ at $16.95 (hardcover) each .... total _____

NYS Sales Tax (Residents only) .... _____

Postage and handling:
$3.50 first book; 1.00 each additional book .... _____

Total enclosed .... _____

Name: _____

Address: _____

City/State/Zip: _____

Phone: (   ) _____

Thank You for your order. Please allow 6–8 weeks for delivery.

Remove form, fold, enclose check, seal on three sides with tape and mail.

Place
Stamp
Here

Golden Heritage Press, Inc.
Suite 25D
500 West 43rd Street
New York, NY 10036